165

HALLOWEEN

JOKES FOR KIDS

A Message From the Publisher

Hello! My name is Hayden and I am the owner of Hayden Fox Publishing, the publishing house that brought you this title.

My hope is that you and your young comedian love this book and enjoy every single page. If you do, please think about **giving us your honest feedback via a review on Amazon**. It may only take a moment, but it really does mean the world for small businesses like mine.

Even if you happen to not like this title, please let us know the reason in your review so that we may improve this title for the future and serve you better.

The mission of Hayden Fox is to create premium content for children that will help them increase their confidence and grow their imaginations while having tons of fun along the way.

Without you, however, this would not be possible, so we sincerely thank you for your purchase and for supporting our company mission.

Sincerely,
Hayden Fox

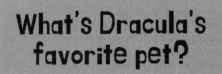

What does Tweety say when trick or treating?

Twick or tweet

Which one of Count Dracula's relatives has a bill and webbed feet?

Count Duckula

What is Dracula's favorite building in New York City?

The Vampire State Building

What do vampires fear the most?

Tooth decay

How come the pirate bought his earring at the dollar store?

Because it was a buck-an-ear!

What is a pirate always looking for even though it's right behind him?

Booty

Why didn't the skeleton score any goals?

Because he had no heart.

Which monster likes to play tricks on Halloween?

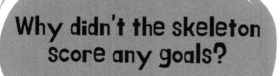

Prankenstein

What's big and scary and has 3 wheels?

A monster riding a tricycle!

What position do zombies play in hockey?

Ghoulie

What did the kids say when they had to choose between their tricycles and candies?

Trike or treat

What instrument does a skeleton play?

The trombone

Who did the ghoul invite to his birthday party?

Anyone he could dig up!

What kind of cookies do monsters prefer?

Ghoul scout cookies

What do you call a monster with a broken leg?

Hoblin Goblin

What do zombies like to drink on a hot summer day?

Ghoul-aid

What do ghosts like to eat for dinner?

Spookghetti

What's a ghost's favorite fruit?

Booberries

Where do vampires usually eat lunch?

At the casketeria.

Why was the ghoul such a messy eater?

Because he was always goblin!

What monster loves dance music?

The Boogieman

Why do ghosts like going out so much?

Because they love to boo-gie!

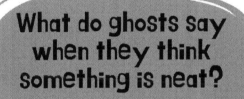

What do ghosts say when they think something is neat?

"Wow, that's ghoul!"

Why was the ghost arrested for scaring youngsters?

Because he didn't have a haunting license!

Where did the zombie throw the football?

Over the ghoul line!

What do you call a ghost who gets too close to the fire?

A toasty ghosty

Where do most of the
werewolves live?

Howllywood,
California

Where do most
goblins live?

North and
South
Scarolina

How do vampires flirt?

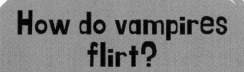

They bat their eyes!

Why doesn't anyone like Dracula?

Because he has a bat temper!

Who does Dracula get letters from?

From his fang club!

Why did the vampire need cold medicine?

In order to stop coffin!

What can't you give the headless horseman?

A headache

Why did the headless horseman go start a business?

He wanted to get a-head in life!

Where do ghosts like to go on vacation?

Mali-boo

Where can you find a witch's garage?

In the broom closet!

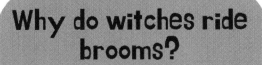

Why do witches ride brooms?

Because the vacuum cleaner's power chord is too short!

Why don't angry witches ride their brooms?

They're afraid of flying off the handle!

How come Dracula never got married?

He never met the right ghoul!

Who did Dracula take to the movies?

His ghoul-friend

What do owls say when they go trick or treating?

Happy Owl-ween!

Where do ghosts use their boats?

The Eerie Canal

Who are a werewolf's cousins?

What-wolf, who-wolf, when-wolf and how-wolf!

Where do werewolves store their belongings?

In a were-house

What do werewolves read to their children before sleeping?

Hairy tails

What do Italian ghosts eat for dinner?

Spookghetti

What do the monsters use to clean the ice after hockey games?

A Zombieoni

What was the mummy musician's favorite note?

The dead sea

How can monsters tell their futures?

By reading their horrorscopes!

What amusement park ride do ghosts like the most?

Roller ghosters

How do ghosts like their coffee?

2 sugars and 2 screams!

Why can't you see a ghost's mother and father?

Because they're transparents!

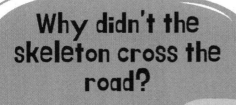

Why didn't the skeleton cross the road?

He didn't have the guts!

What happened to the witch with the upside down nose?

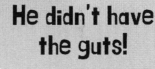

Her hat blew off every time she sneezed!

What do monkey ghosts like to eat?

Boonanas

What sport do vampires like the most?

Batminton

Why can't skeleton musicians perform at church?

Because they have no organs!

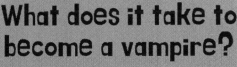

What does it take to become a vampire?

Deadication

Why did the zombie quit his teaching job?

Because he only had 1 pupil left!

Who do cowboy zombies fight?

The Deadskins

What kind of vehicle do zombies drive?

Monster trucks

What did the zombie say after eating the comedian?

This tastes funny!

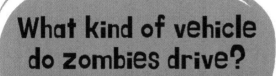

Why did the
zombie join
the army?

He heard they
gave out arms!

Why didn't the
zombie get the role
in the movie?

The director wanted
someone more lively!

What's black, white and dead all over?

A zombie penguin

Why did the zombie comedian get Booed off stage?

Because all his jokes were rotten!

Knock Knock!
Who's there?
Ice Cream.
Ice cream who?
Ice cream every time I see a ghost!

Knock Knock!
Who's there?
Olive.
Olive who?
Olive Halloween!

Knock Knock!
Who's there?
Frank.
Frank who?
Frankenstein!

Knock Knock!
Who's there?
Howl!
Howl who?
Howl you be dressing up this Halloween?

Knock Knock!
Who's there?
Boo.
Boo Who?
Ah, don't cry,
Halloween is just
around the corner!

Knock Knock!
Who's there?
Ivan.
Ivan who?
Ivan to suck
your blood!

Knock Knock!
Who's there?
Phillip.
Phillip who?
Phillip my bag with
Halloween candy!

Knock Knock!
Who's there?
Jacklyn.
Jacklyn who?
Jacklyn Hyde!

Knock Knock!
Who's there?
Essen!
Essen who?
Essen it fun to listen to these Halloween jokes!

Knock Knock!
Who's there?
Iran!
Iran who?
Iran over here to get some candy!

Knock Knock!
Who's there?
Voodoo!
Voodoo who?
Voodoo you
think you are!

Thank you for
reading and
Happy Halloween!

Leave Your Feedback on Amazon

Please think about leaving some feedback via a review on Amazon. It may only take a moment, but it really does mean the world for small businesses like mine.

Even if you did not enjoy this title, please let us know the reason(s) in your review so that we may improve this title and serve you better.

From the Publisher

Hayden Fox's mission is to create premium content for children that will help them expand their vocabulary, grow their imaginations, gain confidence, and share tons of laughs along the way.

Without you, however, this would not be possible, so we sincerely thank you for your purchase and for supporting our company mission.